1.

- - 1

Summary...2

Chapter 1: Introduction to Thrillers.............................4

Chapter 2: Building Suspense 11

Chapter 3: Crafting Thrilling Plots.........................17

Chapter 4: Unpredictable Twists and Turns 24

Chapter 5: Psychological Thrillers 30

Chapter 6: Psychological Thrillers 36

Synopsis..43

2.

3.

4.

5.

6.

7.

8.

9.

Summary

Chapter 1: Introduction to Thrillers

1.1 Definition and Characteristics of Thrillers

1.2 Elements of a Thrilling Plot

1.3 The Importance of Unexpected Twists

Chapter 2: Building Suspense

2.1 Creating Tension through Pacing and Timing

2.2 Developing Intriguing Characters

2.3 Utilizing Setting to Enhance Suspense

Chapter 3: Crafting Thrilling Plots

3.1 Plotting Techniques for Maximum Impact

3.2 Incorporating Red Herrings and Misdirections

3.3 Balancing Action and Psychological Thrills

Chapter 4: Unpredictable Twists and Turns

4.1 Foreshadowing and Subtle Clues

4.2 Shocking Revelations and Betrayals

4.3 Manipulating Reader Expectations

Chapter 5: Psychological Thrillers

5.1 Exploring the Depths of the Human Mind

5.2 Unreliable Narrators and Mind Games

5.3 Delving into Dark Secrets and Obsessions

Chapter 6: Psychological Thrillers

6.1 Exploring the Depths of the Human Mind

6.2 Unreliable Narrators and Mind Games

6.3 Delving into Dark Secrets and Obsessions

Chapter 1: Introduction to Thrillers

Definition of Thrillers

Thrillers are a genre of fiction that elicits excitement, tension, and anticipation in the audience. They typically involve high stakes, danger, and suspenseful plot twists that keep readers or viewers on the edge of their seats. Unlike traditional mysteries where the focus is on solving a puzzle, thrillers emphasize the emotional experience of fear and excitement.

One defining characteristic of thrillers is their ability to provoke intense emotions such as fear, anxiety, or excitement in the audience. This emotional rollercoaster often stems from the protagonist's confrontation with a formidable antagonist or a life-threatening situation. The fast-paced nature of thrillers also contributes to this heightened sense of tension and suspense.

Thrillers can encompass various subgenres such as psychological thrillers, political thrillers, legal thrillers, or action thrillers. Each subgenre brings its unique elements to the table while still adhering to the core characteristics of the thriller genre. For example, psychological thrillers delve into the complexities of human psychology and often feature unreliable narrators or mind-bending plot twists.

Characteristics of Thrillers

One key characteristic of thrillers is the presence of a clear antagonist who poses a significant threat to the protagonist or society at large. This antagonist could be a serial killer, a terrorist organization, or even an internal conflict within the protagonist's own mind. The cat-and-mouse dynamic between the protagonist and antagonist drives much of the narrative tension in thrillers.

Another common feature of thrillers is the element of surprise. Twist endings, unexpected betrayals, and shocking revelations are staples of this genre. These surprises not only keep audiences engaged but also challenge their assumptions about characters and events within the story.

The pacing in thrillers is typically fast-paced, with short chapters or scenes that propel the narrative forward. This rapid tempo creates a sense of urgency and compels readers or viewers to keep turning pages or watching until they reach a resolution. Additionally, cliffhangers at chapter breaks or commercial breaks in films heighten suspense and maintain audience interest.

Elements of a Thrilling Plot

Thrillers are known for their ability to captivate audiences with gripping plots that keep them on the edge of their seats. Several key elements contribute to creating a thrilling plot that hooks readers or viewers from the beginning and keeps them engaged until the very end.

One essential element of a thrilling plot is the concept of high stakes. The protagonist must face significant risks or consequences if they fail to overcome the challenges presented by the antagonist. These stakes can be personal, such as the threat of harm to loved ones, or societal, like preventing a catastrophic event from occurring. By raising the stakes, thrillers create a sense of urgency and tension that propels the narrative forward.

In addition to high stakes, another crucial element is the presence of unexpected plot twists. These twists keep audiences guessing and add layers of complexity to the story. Whether it's a shocking betrayal, a sudden revelation, or an unforeseen turn of events, these surprises inject excitement and unpredictability into the plot. For example, in Gillian Flynn's novel "Gone Girl," the twist involving the disappearance of Amy Dunne adds a new dimension to the story and leaves readers eagerly anticipating what will happen next.

The pacing of a thriller also plays a significant role in creating a compelling plot. Fast-paced action sequences, tense confrontations, and rapid developments keep readers or viewers hooked as they race through each chapter or scene. By maintaining momentum and avoiding lulls in the narrative, thrillers sustain suspense and build towards an explosive climax that delivers on the promises set up earlier in the story.

Furthermore, effective use of foreshadowing can enhance the tension in a thriller plot. By dropping subtle hints or clues about future events early on in the story, authors or filmmakers can create anticipation and intrigue among audiences. When these foreshadowed elements come to fruition later in the plot, it not only provides satisfaction but also reinforces the sense of coherence and clever storytelling within the thriller genre.

The Importance of Unexpected Twists

Unexpected plot twists are a vital component of thrilling narratives, adding depth and intrigue to the story. These twists serve to keep audiences engaged and guessing, preventing predictability and monotony in the plot. By introducing unexpected developments, authors or filmmakers can challenge conventional storytelling norms and deliver a memorable experience for their audience.

One key aspect of unexpected twists is their ability to subvert audience expectations. When a story takes an unforeseen turn, it forces viewers or readers to reevaluate their assumptions about the characters and the narrative trajectory. This element of surprise can lead to heightened emotional reactions, such as shock, excitement, or suspense, enhancing the overall impact of the story.

Moreover, unexpected twists have the power to elevate the complexity of a plot by introducing new layers of conflict or ambiguity. By introducing conflicting motivations, hidden agendas, or moral dilemmas through these twists, storytellers can create multi-dimensional characters and intricate relationships that captivate audiences. For example, in Christopher Nolan's film "The Prestige," the revelation of multiple layers of deception between rival magicians adds a compelling twist that deepens the narrative tension.

Additionally, unexpected twists can serve as a catalyst for character development and growth. When faced with unforeseen challenges or revelations, protagonists are forced to adapt and evolve in response to these changes. This dynamic evolution not only adds depth to the characters but also allows for exploration of themes such as resilience, morality, and personal transformation within the context of the thriller genre.

In conclusion, unexpected plot twists play a crucial role in captivating audiences and elevating the quality of thrilling narratives. By incorporating surprising developments that challenge expectations, deepen complexity, and drive character growth, storytellers can create engaging stories that leave a lasting impression on their audience.

Chapter 2: Building Suspense

Creating Tension through Pacing and Timing

One of the most effective ways to build suspense in a thriller is through the careful manipulation of pacing and timing. By controlling the speed at which events unfold and strategically placing key moments within the narrative, authors and filmmakers can keep audiences on edge and eager to uncover what happens next.

Pacing refers to the rhythm or tempo of a story, determining how quickly or slowly events progress. In thrillers, fast-paced pacing is often used to heighten tension and maintain audience engagement. Quick scene transitions, rapid dialogue exchanges, and action-packed sequences all contribute to a sense of urgency that propels the plot forward. Conversely, slowing down the pace can create moments of anticipation and dread, allowing readers or viewers to savor suspenseful moments before the next twist or revelation.

Timing plays a crucial role in building suspense by strategically revealing information at key points in the story. By delaying critical revelations or plot twists until just the right moment, storytellers can maximize their impact on audiences. For example, unveiling a shocking betrayal or unexpected revelation during a climactic confrontation between the protagonist and antagonist can amplify emotional reactions and keep viewers or readers hooked until the resolution.

Real-world examples of effective use of pacing and timing can be seen in Alfred Hitchcock's classic thriller "Psycho." The film masterfully builds tension through its deliberate pacing, gradually escalating suspense as Marion Crane's actions lead her closer to danger. The infamous shower scene exemplifies Hitchcock's skillful timing, shocking audiences with its sudden violence and unexpected turn of events.

In conclusion, creating tension through pacing and timing is essential for crafting a gripping thriller that keeps audiences on the edge of their seats. By carefully orchestrating the speed at which events unfold and strategically revealing key moments within the narrative, storytellers can enhance suspense, engage viewers or readers, and deliver a memorable storytelling experience.

Developing Intriguing Characters

Creating compelling and intriguing characters is essential for building suspense in a thriller. Characters drive the narrative, and their actions, motivations, and relationships can significantly impact the tension and intrigue of the story.

One way to develop intriguing characters is to give them depth and complexity. Avoid one-dimensional stereotypes and instead craft characters with layers, flaws, and conflicting desires. This complexity adds richness to the story and keeps readers or viewers guessing about the character's true intentions.

Another effective technique is to introduce ambiguity into your characters. By keeping certain aspects of a character's past or motivations shrouded in mystery, you can create a sense of unease and uncertainty that adds to the overall suspense. For example, a seemingly trustworthy character may have hidden agendas or dark secrets that are gradually revealed throughout the story.

Real-world examples of intriguing characters can be found in novels like Gillian Flynn's "Gone Girl" or films like "The Sixth Sense." In both cases, the main characters are complex individuals with hidden depths that slowly unravel as the plot progresses. These revelations not only surprise audiences but also deepen their investment in the story.

To further enhance character intrigue, consider incorporating moral ambiguity into your protagonists or antagonists. Characters who operate in shades of gray rather than black-and-white morality can challenge audience expectations and keep them on edge as they navigate ethical dilemmas and conflicting loyalties.

In conclusion, developing intriguing characters is crucial for building suspense in a thriller. By creating complex, ambiguous, and morally nuanced characters, storytellers can captivate audiences, drive the narrative forward, and keep readers or viewers eagerly anticipating each twist and turn in the story.

Utilizing Setting to Enhance Suspense

Setting plays a crucial role in creating suspense in a thriller. By carefully crafting the environment where the story unfolds, writers can heighten tension, evoke mood, and keep readers or viewers on edge throughout the narrative.

One way to utilize setting effectively is to establish a sense of isolation or confinement. Placing characters in remote locations, such as a deserted island, an abandoned house, or a snow-covered mountain, can create a feeling of vulnerability and helplessness. This isolation intensifies the suspense as characters are cut off from external help or resources, forcing them to confront their fears and adversaries head-on.

Furthermore, using atmospheric descriptions can enhance the overall mood and atmosphere of the story. Describing eerie landscapes, ominous weather patterns, or decaying buildings can instill a sense of foreboding in readers or viewers. The setting itself becomes a character in the narrative, influencing the actions and decisions of the protagonists and adding layers of complexity to the plot.

Incorporating elements of unpredictability into the setting can also ramp up suspense. Introducing sudden changes in weather conditions, unexpected obstacles, or hidden dangers lurking within familiar surroundings keeps audiences guessing and maintains a high level of tension throughout the story. This unpredictability adds an element of surprise that keeps readers or viewers engaged and eager to uncover what will happen next.

Real-world examples like Stephen King's "The Shining," set in an isolated hotel during a snowstorm, effectively use setting to enhance suspense. The eerie atmosphere created by the remote location and supernatural occurrences contributes significantly to the overall sense of dread and anticipation experienced by both characters and audience.

Chapter 3: Crafting Thrilling Plots

Plotting Techniques for Maximum Impact

Creating a thrilling plot that captivates readers or viewers requires careful consideration of various techniques to maximize impact. From clever twists to well-paced revelations, crafting a plot that keeps audiences on the edge of their seats is essential for a successful thriller.

Clever Plot Twists

One of the most effective ways to keep audiences engaged and surprised is through clever plot twists. These unexpected turns in the story can subvert expectations, challenge assumptions, and add layers of complexity to the narrative. To create impactful plot twists, foreshadowing is key. By subtly hinting at future developments without giving away the surprise, storytellers can build anticipation and set the stage for a shocking revelation.

Real-world examples like Agatha Christie's "And Then There Were None" showcase how skillful use of plot twists can elevate a thriller. The novel's intricate web of deception and unexpected reveals keeps readers guessing until the very end, delivering a satisfying payoff that lingers long after the final page.

Layered Storytelling

Incorporating multiple layers into your plot can add depth and richness to your storytelling. By weaving together different subplots, character arcs, and thematic elements, you can create a multi-dimensional narrative that engages audiences on various levels. Each layer should contribute to the overall suspense and intrigue of the story, building towards a climactic resolution that ties all threads together.

An excellent example of layered storytelling can be seen in Christopher Nolan's film "Inception." The movie's complex structure, with its dream within a dream concept and overlapping timelines, immerses viewers in a maze of intrigue and uncertainty. As each layer unfolds, new revelations emerge, keeping audiences enthralled until the mind-bending conclusion.

Suspenseful Climaxes

The climax of a thriller is where all the tension and suspense built throughout the story culminate in a dramatic showdown or revelation. To maximize impact, ensure that your climax delivers on the promises made earlier in the plot. Whether it's an intense action sequence, a shocking twist, or a moral dilemma with far-reaching consequences, make sure that the climax leaves audiences breathless and eager for resolution.

A classic example of an unforgettable climax can be found in Alfred Hitchcock's "Vertigo." The film's gripping finale not only resolves the central mystery but also delves into complex themes of obsession and identity. By combining emotional depth with pulse-pounding suspense, Hitchcock creates a climax that resonates long after the credits roll.

Incorporating Red Herrings and Misdirections

One of the key elements in crafting a thrilling plot is the strategic use of red herrings and misdirections. These narrative devices are designed to lead audiences down false paths, creating suspense and uncertainty as they try to unravel the mystery. By planting misleading clues or introducing deceptive characters, storytellers can keep readers or viewers guessing until the final reveal.

Red herrings are particularly effective in diverting attention away from the true culprit or resolution of the story. They can be subtle details that seem significant but ultimately lead nowhere, or they can be more overt misdirections that point towards a false conclusion. Skillful use of red herrings can heighten tension, increase intrigue, and make the eventual revelation even more satisfying.

An example of masterful incorporation of red herrings can be found in Gillian Flynn's novel "Gone Girl." Throughout the story, Flynn expertly plants misleading clues and introduces unreliable narrators to keep readers on their toes. The shifting perspectives and conflicting accounts create a sense of doubt and suspicion, making it challenging for audiences to discern the truth amidst all the deception.

Misdirections, on the other hand, involve steering audiences towards a false interpretation of events or characters. This technique plays with expectations and assumptions, leading viewers or readers to draw incorrect conclusions based on manipulated information. By skillfully manipulating perceptions and playing with audience expectations, storytellers can craft intricate plots that surprise and engage their audience.

A classic example of incorporating misdirections is seen in Alfred Hitchcock's film "Psycho." Through clever editing techniques and misleading character portrayals, Hitchcock leads viewers down unexpected paths before delivering a shocking twist that upends everything they thought they knew about the story. The careful manipulation of information keeps audiences on edge and enhances the impact of the eventual revelation.

Balancing Action and Psychological Thrills

When crafting a thrilling plot, it is essential to strike a balance between action-packed sequences and psychological thrills. While action scenes can provide excitement and adrenaline, psychological elements delve into the characters' minds, emotions, and motivations, adding depth and complexity to the narrative.

One way to achieve this balance is by intertwining action with psychological tension. For example, in a high-stakes chase scene, incorporating internal monologues or flashbacks that reveal the character's fears or past traumas can heighten the emotional stakes and create a more immersive experience for the audience. This combination of physical danger and psychological turmoil keeps viewers on the edge of their seats while also investing them emotionally in the characters' journeys.

Another effective strategy is to use action as a catalyst for psychological exploration. When characters are thrust into intense situations that test their limits, it provides an opportunity to delve into their psyche, showcasing their strengths, vulnerabilities, and inner conflicts. By using action as a backdrop for character development, storytellers can create multidimensional protagonists who resonate with audiences on a deeper level.

An excellent example of balancing action and psychological thrills can be seen in Christopher Nolan's film "Inception." The movie seamlessly weaves together mind-bending action sequences with complex emotional arcs, exploring themes of guilt, grief, and redemption amidst the high-octane heist plot. By blending heart-pounding set pieces with introspective character moments, Nolan creates a gripping narrative that resonates both intellectually and emotionally with viewers.

Chapter 4: Unpredictable Twists and Turns

Foreshadowing and Subtle Clues

Foreshadowing is a powerful storytelling technique that involves hinting at future events or developments in a subtle manner. By planting clues early on in the narrative, writers can build anticipation, create suspense, and prepare audiences for upcoming twists or revelations. Effective foreshadowing not only adds depth to the story but also enhances the impact of key plot points.

One classic example of foreshadowing can be found in J.K. Rowling's "Harry Potter" series. Throughout the books, Rowling drops subtle hints about important events or character motivations that will play a significant role later in the story. For instance, the presence of a certain symbol or recurring theme may foreshadow a major plot twist or character arc, keeping readers engaged and eager to uncover the hidden connections.

Moreover, foreshadowing can also be used to create a sense of inevitability or irony in the narrative. By subtly suggesting future outcomes without explicitly revealing them, writers can add layers of complexity to their storytelling and deepen the emotional impact of key moments. This technique allows audiences to feel more invested in the story as they anticipate how events will unfold based on the clues provided.

In addition to foreshadowing, incorporating subtle clues throughout the plot can further engage audiences and enhance their experience. These clues may come in various forms, such as cryptic messages, ambiguous dialogue, or seemingly insignificant details that gain significance later on. By paying attention to these subtle hints, readers or viewers can piece together information and make connections that lead to a deeper understanding of the story.

An excellent illustration of using subtle clues effectively is seen in Agatha Christie's mystery novel "Murder on the Orient Express." Throughout the book, Christie strategically places small details and seemingly inconsequential observations that ultimately converge towards a surprising conclusion. Readers who pick up on these subtle clues are rewarded with a greater appreciation for Christie's masterful plotting and clever misdirection.

Shocking Revelations and Betrayals

One of the most captivating elements in storytelling is the introduction of shocking revelations and betrayals that completely alter the course of a narrative. These unexpected twists not only surprise audiences but also challenge their perceptions of characters, events, and relationships within the story.

Shocking revelations often serve as pivotal moments that redefine the audience's understanding of the plot. For example, in George R.R. Martin's "A Song of Ice and Fire" series, the revelation of Jon Snow's true parentage fundamentally changes how readers view his character and his place in the larger political landscape of Westeros. This type of revelation can create a ripple effect throughout the story, leading to new conflicts, alliances, and motivations among characters.

Betrayals, on the other hand, introduce a sense of betrayal or deception that can shatter trust and relationships within a narrative. A classic example can be found in William Shakespeare's "Julius Caesar," where Brutus betrays Caesar by joining the conspiracy to assassinate him. This act not only leads to Caesar's downfall but also sets off a chain reaction of betrayals and tragedies that ultimately shape the fate of Rome.

What makes shocking revelations and betrayals so compelling is their ability to subvert expectations and challenge conventional storytelling tropes. When well-executed, these twists can leave audiences reeling with disbelief while simultaneously deepening their engagement with the narrative. Whether it's a long-lost sibling revealing themselves or a trusted ally turning against the protagonist, these moments have the power to keep viewers or readers on the edge of their seats.

In conclusion, shocking revelations and betrayals are essential tools for storytellers looking to inject drama, suspense, and complexity into their narratives. By carefully crafting these twists and turns, writers can keep audiences guessing while delivering unforgettable moments that resonate long after the story has ended.

Manipulating Reader Expectations

One of the most powerful tools in a writer's arsenal is the ability to manipulate reader expectations. By setting up certain assumptions or patterns and then subverting them, authors can create moments of shock, surprise, and intrigue that keep audiences engaged.

One way to manipulate reader expectations is through the use of foreshadowing. By dropping subtle hints or clues throughout the narrative, writers can lead readers down a particular path only to pull the rug out from under them with a surprising twist. For example, in Agatha Christie's "And Then There Were None," the author expertly plants seeds of doubt and suspicion among the characters, keeping readers guessing until the very end when the true culprit is revealed.

Another technique is misdirection, where writers intentionally draw attention away from important details or events to create a sense of surprise when they are finally revealed. This can be seen in Christopher Nolan's film "The Prestige," where he uses non-linear storytelling to keep viewers guessing about the true nature of the rivalry between two magicians until a shocking revelation changes everything they thought they knew.

Furthermore, playing with character archetypes can also manipulate reader expectations. By presenting characters who initially fit into familiar tropes but then subverting those expectations by revealing hidden depths or motivations, writers can challenge preconceived notions and keep audiences on their toes. For instance, in Gillian Flynn's "Gone Girl," the protagonist Amy Dunne initially appears as a victim but later reveals herself to be a master manipulator, completely changing how readers perceive her character.

In conclusion, manipulating reader expectations is an essential skill for storytellers looking to create compelling narratives that surprise and captivate audiences. By using techniques like foreshadowing, misdirection, and playing with character archetypes, writers can craft stories that keep readers guessing until the very last page.

Chapter 5: Psychological Thrillers

Exploring the Depths of the Human Mind

Delving into the intricacies of the human mind is a fascinating journey that psychological thrillers often undertake. By exploring the depths of characters' thoughts, emotions, and motivations, these stories offer a unique insight into the complexities of human behavior and psyche.

One aspect that psychological thrillers often explore is the concept of moral ambiguity. Characters in these narratives are frequently faced with difficult choices that blur the lines between right and wrong, forcing audiences to question their own ethical beliefs and values. For example, in Fyodor Dostoevsky's "Crime and Punishment," the protagonist Raskolnikov grapples with his conscience after committing a murder, leading readers to ponder the nature of guilt, redemption, and morality.

Furthermore, psychological thrillers often delve into themes of identity and self-discovery. Characters may undergo profound transformations or confront hidden truths about themselves that challenge their perceptions of reality. In Patricia Highsmith's "The Talented Mr. Ripley," the protagonist Tom Ripley navigates a web of deceit and manipulation as he grapples with his own insecurities and desires, ultimately blurring the lines between his true self and his fabricated persona.

In addition to individual character exploration, psychological thrillers also shed light on interpersonal dynamics and relationships. Whether it's examining toxic friendships, dysfunctional families, or manipulative partnerships, these stories offer a glimpse into the intricate web of connections that shape human interactions. Gillian Flynn's "Sharp Objects" delves into the complex relationship between mother and daughter, unraveling dark secrets and deep-seated traumas that impact their bond.

Overall, exploring the depths of the human mind in psychological thrillers provides audiences with a thought-provoking experience that challenges preconceived notions about human nature. By delving into moral dilemmas, identity crises, and complex relationships, these stories offer a nuanced portrayal of human behavior that resonates long after the final page or screen fades to black.

Unreliable Narrators

Unreliable narrators are a common device used in psychological thrillers to create suspense, mystery, and intrigue. These narrators may intentionally deceive the audience or themselves, leading to a distorted perception of reality within the story. By casting doubt on the reliability of the narrator, authors can manipulate readers' perceptions and challenge their ability to discern truth from fiction.

One classic example of an unreliable narrator is found in Gillian Flynn's "Gone Girl." The protagonist, Amy Dunne, presents her version of events through diary entries that gradually reveal inconsistencies and manipulations. As readers uncover the layers of deception woven by Amy, they are forced to question her credibility and motives, adding complexity to the narrative.

Unreliable narrators can also be used to explore themes of memory distortion and psychological trauma. In Paula Hawkins' "The Girl on the Train," the protagonist Rachel suffers from alcohol-induced blackouts that cloud her recollection of past events. Her fragmented memories and unreliable narration create a sense of unease and uncertainty, mirroring her own internal struggles with guilt and self-doubt.

Mind Games

Mind games play a crucial role in psychological thrillers by manipulating characters' perceptions, motivations, and actions. These games often involve psychological manipulation, gaslighting, or elaborate schemes designed to confuse or control others. By engaging in mind games, characters challenge each other's sanity, morality, and trustworthiness, creating tension and suspense throughout the narrative.

In Dennis Lehane's "Shutter Island," the protagonist Teddy Daniels finds himself embroiled in a complex web of mind games orchestrated by both external forces and his own psyche. As he unravels the mysteries surrounding Shutter Island's psychiatric hospital, Teddy must navigate through layers of deception and illusion that blur the lines between reality and delusion.

Mind games can also be used to explore power dynamics within relationships. In Sarah Pinborough's "Behind Her Eyes," the characters engage in a twisted game of manipulation and betrayal that culminates in a shocking revelation. Through strategic maneuvers and psychological warfare, the protagonists challenge each other's perceptions of truth and loyalty, leading to a climactic showdown that leaves readers questioning everything they thought they knew.

Delving into Dark Secrets and Obsessions

Exploring dark secrets and obsessions is a common theme in psychological thrillers, adding layers of complexity to characters and driving the narrative forward. These hidden truths and fixations often serve as catalysts for suspense, intrigue, and psychological tension within the story.

In Patricia Highsmith's "The Talented Mr. Ripley," the protagonist Tom Ripley harbors a deep-seated obsession with wealth, status, and identity. His relentless pursuit of these desires leads him down a dark path of deception, manipulation, and murder. As Tom delves deeper into his own twisted psyche, his secrets unravel, exposing the lengths he is willing to go to maintain his facade.

Dark secrets can also manifest in familial relationships, as seen in Ruth Ware's "The Turn of the Key." The protagonist Rowan Caine takes on a nanny position at a remote estate with a history of tragedy. As she uncovers the family's hidden past and dark secrets, Rowan becomes entangled in a web of lies and deceit that threaten her sanity and safety. Her obsession with uncovering the truth propels her towards a chilling revelation that changes everything she thought she knew.

Obsessions can drive characters to extreme lengths, blurring the lines between right and wrong. In Tana French's "In the Woods," detective Rob Ryan becomes consumed by his childhood trauma and an unsolved murder case that haunts him. His relentless pursuit of answers leads him down a dangerous path where his own obsessions threaten to unravel his sanity and jeopardize his relationships. As Rob delves deeper into the darkness within himself, he must confront his inner demons to solve the mystery before it consumes him entirely.

Chapter 6: Psychological Thrillers

Exploring the Depths of the Human Mind

Psychological thrillers offer a captivating exploration of the human mind, delving into the intricate layers of characters' thoughts, emotions, and motivations. These stories provide a unique insight into the complexities of human behavior and psyche, challenging audiences to question their own beliefs and values.

One fascinating aspect that psychological thrillers often delve into is moral ambiguity. Characters are frequently placed in situations where they must navigate through difficult choices that blur the lines between right and wrong. For instance, in "Gone Girl" by Gillian Flynn, both protagonists manipulate truths to suit their narratives, leaving readers questioning traditional notions of morality and ethics.

Moreover, these stories often touch upon themes of identity and self-discovery. Characters may undergo profound transformations or confront hidden truths about themselves that challenge their perceptions of reality. In "Black Swan," Nina Sayers grapples with her dual identity as she descends into madness while pursuing perfection in ballet.

In addition to individual character exploration, psychological thrillers shed light on complex interpersonal dynamics and relationships. Whether it's toxic friendships or manipulative partnerships, these narratives offer a glimpse into the intricate web of connections that shape human interactions. In "The Girl on the Train," Rachel's obsession with her ex-husband's new life leads her down a path of self-destruction fueled by jealousy and insecurity.

Unreliable Narrators

The use of unreliable narrators is a powerful tool in psychological thrillers to create suspense and intrigue by distorting reality within the narrative. By casting doubt on the credibility of the narrator, authors can manipulate readers' perceptions and challenge their ability to discern truth from fiction.

An excellent example is found in Agatha Christie's "The Murder of Roger Ackroyd," where the narrator conceals crucial information from readers until the shocking reveal at the end. This manipulation keeps readers engaged as they try to unravel the mystery alongside the unreliable narrator.

Unreliable narrators can also be used to explore themes of memory distortion and mental health issues. In "Fight Club" by Chuck Palahniuk, the protagonist suffers from dissociative identity disorder, leading to conflicting narratives that blur reality for both him and the audience.

Mind Games

Mind games are a staple in psychological thrillers, involving manipulation tactics that challenge characters' perceptions and actions. These games often revolve around power dynamics, control, and deception, creating tension and suspense throughout the narrative.

In "The Silence of The Lambs," Dr. Hannibal Lecter engages in elaborate mind games with FBI agent Clarice Starling as he manipulates her vulnerabilities to extract information. The psychological warfare between them adds depth to their interactions and keeps readers on edge.

Mind games can also explore themes of trust and betrayal within relationships. In "Gone Girl," Amy orchestrates an intricate plan to frame her husband for her disappearance, playing mind games not only with him but also with readers who struggle to decipher her true intentions.

Unreliable Narrators

Unreliable narrators are a common and effective technique used in psychological thrillers to manipulate readers' perceptions and create suspense. By presenting a narrator whose credibility is questionable, authors can lead audiences down unexpected paths and challenge their ability to discern truth from fiction.

In the novel "The Girl on the Train" by Paula Hawkins, the protagonist Rachel suffers from alcohol-induced blackouts, making her recollection of events unreliable. This unreliable narration adds layers of complexity to the story as readers must piece together the truth from fragmented memories and distorted perceptions.

Furthermore, unreliable narrators can serve as a vehicle for exploring themes of deception and manipulation. In "We Need to Talk About Kevin" by Lionel Shriver, the narrator Eva struggles with guilt and denial about her son's violent actions. Her biased perspective skews the narrative, forcing readers to question her reliability and motivations.

Mind Games

Mind games play a crucial role in psychological thrillers, involving intricate manipulation tactics that challenge characters' beliefs and actions. These games often revolve around power dynamics, control, and psychological warfare, adding layers of tension and suspense to the narrative.

In the movie "Inception," director Christopher Nolan explores mind games through the concept of shared dreaming. The characters navigate through layers of dreams within dreams, manipulating perceptions and realities to achieve their objectives. This complex interplay between illusion and reality keeps viewers engaged in a constant state of uncertainty.

Moreover, mind games can also delve into themes of gaslighting and psychological manipulation within relationships. In "Gaslight," a classic psychological

thriller film, a husband manipulates his wife into
questioning her sanity by altering small details in their
environment. This insidious form of mind game
highlights how subtle tactics can have profound effects
on one's mental well-being.

Delving into Dark Secrets and Obsessions

Exploring dark secrets and obsessions is a common
theme in psychological thrillers, adding layers of
complexity to characters and driving the narrative
forward. These hidden truths and fixations often serve
as catalysts for suspense, intrigue, and psychological
tension within the story.

In the novel "Gone Girl" by Gillian Flynn, the
protagonist Amy's dark secret of faking her own
disappearance to frame her husband for murder sets off
a chain of events that unravel their marriage. The
obsession with maintaining a perfect facade and
seeking revenge drives Amy to extreme lengths,
blurring the lines between reality and deception.

Furthermore, delving into dark secrets can also shed
light on characters' vulnerabilities and inner demons.
In the TV series "Big Little Lies," each character

harbors secrets that slowly unravel throughout the season, exposing their fears, traumas, and insecurities. These hidden truths not only drive the plot but also deepen our understanding of human nature and the complexities of relationships.

Obsessions, on the other hand, can manifest in various forms in psychological thrillers, from fixation on a person to an idea or a goal. In Alfred Hitchcock's film "Vertigo," the protagonist Scottie's obsessive desire to recreate his lost love through another woman leads him down a path of manipulation and tragedy. His relentless pursuit of an unattainable ideal showcases how obsessions can consume one's identity and sanity.

Moreover, exploring dark secrets and obsessions can also serve as a reflection of societal taboos or forbidden desires. In Patricia Highsmith's novel "The Talented Mr. Ripley," the protagonist Tom Ripley's obsession with wealth and status drives him to commit heinous acts to maintain his facade. This exploration of greed, envy, and deceit highlights how societal pressures can push individuals towards darker impulses.

Synopsis: Title: L'Ã‰nigme de Minuit

Description: Write a thriller with thrilling plots and unexpected twists.

Synopsis: "L'Ã‰nigme de Minuit" is a gripping thriller that will keep readers on the edge of their seats with its thrilling plots and unexpected twists. The story follows a detective who is tasked with solving a mysterious murder case that takes place at midnight. As he delves deeper into the investigation, he uncovers dark secrets and hidden motives that lead him down a dangerous path filled with suspense and danger.

The book explores themes of deception, betrayal, and the lengths people will go to protect their secrets. The detective must navigate through a web of lies and deceit to uncover the truth behind the murder, all while facing threats from unknown adversaries who will stop at nothing to keep their secrets hidden.

With its fast-paced narrative and complex characters, "L'Ã‰nigme de Minuit" keeps readers guessing until the very end. The author skillfully weaves together multiple storylines and plot twists that will leave readers shocked and eager to unravel the mystery alongside the detective.

Overall, "L'Ã‰nigme de Minuit" is a thrilling read that will appeal to fans of suspenseful thrillers looking for an engaging and unpredictable story filled with twists and turns.